THE READER'S DIGEST
KEYBOARD COURSE

LEARN TO PLAY 100 UNFORGETTABLE SONGS THE EASY WAY

THE READER'S DIGEST ASSOCIATION, INC.
New York, NY / Montreal

First printing in paperback 2012

Copyright © 2005 The Reader's Digest Association, Inc.
All rights reserved. Unauthorized reproduction, in any manner, is prohibited.

ISBN: 978-1-60652-039-0 (hardcover)
ISBN: 978-1-60652-428-2 (paperback)

Previously published in 1991 as *The Easy Way to Play 100 Unforgettable Hits*
Reader's Digest is a registered trademark of The Reader's Digest Association, Inc.

7 9 10 8 6   (hardcover)
1 3 5 7 9 10 8 6 4 2   (paperback)

Printed in China

THE EASY WAY TO PLAY
100 UNFORGETTABLE HITS

Index to Sections

Index to Songs

How This Book Helps You to Play Real Music

We believe that anyone—well, *almost* anyone—can play music. And we believe that with this songbook, more people than ever before will be able to sit down and plunk out some of the best popular songs ever written.

THE READER'S DIGEST KEYBOARD COURSE has been designed primarily for two groups of people: those who have very limited piano skills and those who enjoy the electronic keyboard. If you play another instrument, you can use the book too, as you'll see when you read on. Whatever the instrument, everything is designed to let you play the melodies you know and love with the very least effort and with the utmost comfort and convenience.

To start with, there are the 100 melodies themselves. Every song in this book is, indeed, an unforgettable hit. All have been performed and recorded by many different stylists, both vocal and instrumental, and by different types of orchestras, from swing to sweet to symphonic. You'll find the glorious melodies and lyrics of such composers as George and Ira Gershwin, Richard Rogers and Oscar Hammerstein, Cole Porter,

Walter Donaldson, Jerome Kern, Alan Jay Lerner and Frederick Loewe, and Irving Berlin.

You will find just a few contemporary songs here. The reason for that is that many recent songs don't translate comfortably to a solo piano or keyboard: Their complex rhythms and bass guitar lines can't be duplicated without considerable effort, and the electronic effects that can be produced on a recording cannot be approximated. All of the songs here stand on their own as *melodies*.

The songs that we have included are songs that have endured, and will continue to endure, for generations. And all have been made easy—and fun—to play by Dan Fox, the master arranger of every Reader's Digest music book. All sound full and rich.

Now read on a bit, take a quick look at the few sample bars of "As Time Goes By" printed below and discover just how this book can work for you.

Keyboard players! Anything printed in blue is especially for you
Black print is for easy piano and more experienced players

Copyright © 1931 (Renewed) Warner Bros. Inc.

For Electronic Keyboards

Anything printed in blue is designed especially for you. This includes the top line of the music — the treble, or right-hand, clef — with the notes numbered for those who can't read music, as well as the suggested tempos, rhythms and colors (more about these later). Of course, if you can play the piano and use your electronic keyboard with both hands, just as you do an acoustic piano keyboard, it's advisable to play the full-scored piano arrangements for bass and treble clefs, printed in black. See the section on "Easy Piano" that follows for further information.

For chords to accompany the melody, look to the letters, also printed in blue, above the keyboard line. (The simplest, inexpensive monophonic [one-note-at-a-time] models of keyboard will not play chords.) For this and other instructions, *please consult the manual that came with your instrument.* The notes that can sound automatic chords will probably be identified on the backboard behind the keys of your instrument. But to help you find them, you can use the peel-off stickers with letter names that are provided with this book. (See "About the Stickers" on the following page.) You don't have to know what notes constitute each chord; just press the indicated key with your left hand. For a simple major chord you usually press one key or button. For example, to play a C chord, press a C in the designated bass portion of the keyboard, below Middle C. That

key will automatically play the three notes of a C chord (C, E and G). If you want a D chord (D-F♯-A), just press a D. To play minor chords or major and minor 7th chords (indicated in the music by such notations as Cm, G(7), Gm(7), and so on), you may have to use two, three or four fingers of your left hand. Different makes of keyboards require different techniques. For example, on a Casio, to play a minor chord, such as Cm, you play the C plus any neighboring note directly above the C. On a Yamaha, you would play the C plus any note *below* the C. If your instrument does not play 7th chords, you can still get a satisfactory harmony with the basic chord — say, a G rather than a G(7). In fact, the parentheses around the 7 indicate that the 7th chord is optional. *Again, consult your manual.*

At the top right-hand corner of the first page of each song, we have suggested tempos, rhythms and instrumental colors for that tune. Always remember that our suggestions are just that — *suggestions*. As you become more familiar with the keyboard, you'll begin to experiment with the music, and you'll have fun choosing your own instrumental sounds and different rhythms for a song.

Counting time. If you know how the song goes, you will probably know how long each note should be held — even if you don't know a half-note from a quarter-note. We don't go into musical notation here. However, we do show you where the beats are by the red marks underneath the lyrics; each mark (▾) is to be counted as one beat. Your electronic keyboard probably has a tempo light that blinks on each beat, so you can coordinate with that — one ▾ for each blink.

Automatic rhythms. The rhythms you can use on a song depend on the make and model of your instrument. Some electronic keyboards can play a polka rhythm; others cannot. Some have a "cha-cha" button, others a "bossa nova." Some can combine two rhythms to sound like a rhythm they don't have on a single button. Again, study your manufacturer's manual. And experiment.

Instrumental colors. Most keyboards offer piano, flute, guitar, strings, organ and a few other instrumental sounds, or colors. Some of the more versatile models allow you to mix different colors, which may enable you to come closer to the actual instrument sounds, or even to create your own sounds. Once again, consult your manual, since different makes offer different choices.

Once you know your keyboard and its many possibilities, you may be able to simulate an orchestral arrangement even if you are not a trained musician. Certainly your satisfaction will come easier and faster than you ever dared to dream, and you'll have great fun getting there. And remember, players on electronic instruments have a great advantage: you can play with earphones, and no one has to hear what you're doing until you're ready to turn on the amplifier and dazzle them.

Easy Piano

Perhaps you're a piano student, or a retiree who is "getting back" to the piano after not touching it for most of your adult years. Or you're a wind instrument player who always wanted to "play a little piano." Then our very easy two-hand arrangements, printed in black, are for you. (The melody line, printed in blue, is for electronic keyboards.)

Since some players may have little experience with the bass, or left-hand, clef, our arrangements never ask you to play more than a single note at a time with your left hand. The name of each bass

note is printed in red under the lines, under each note. Until you grow more familiar with the bass notes, you can use the peel-off stickers to identify the notes in the two octaves from Middle C down. You might also find the beat marks (▾), printed in red, helpful.

More experienced players can refer to the chords that we've indicated at the top of the piano lines, in black. These chords are sometimes different from those on the keyboard, or blue, lines, substituting more complex harmonies that are not in the automatic chord bank of electronic keyboards.

For Non-Keyboard Players

If you play a single-note instrument, such as a violin, flute, saxophone, clarinet, oboe, trumpet, harmonica or melodica, you can play from the electronic keyboard melody line (printed in blue), reading the notes. However, if you want to play in combination with another instrument, you would have to be sure that the other instrument is pitched in the same key. Clarinet, trumpet and tenor or soprano saxophone, for example, are B-flat instruments and can play together from the same music. Piano, guitar, accordion, autoharp, violin, flute, oboe and some recorders are in C. Alto and baritone saxophone and mellophone are in E flat, and so on.

If you play accordion or autoharp, you can certainly play from the blue lines; but depending on the options your particular instrument provides, you might get more variety out of the harmonies in the piano staves, printed in black. *Guitarists* can begin with the simpler chords of the blue lines and then graduate to the chords in black.

It's conceivable to us that different members of your household may use these arrangements in different ways at different levels of proficiency — the more the merrier.

Now, let's play the music! And perhaps you'd like to start with our musical illustration, the timeless "As Time Goes By." Go ahead, try it. See if Dooley Wilson, who played it in *Casablanca*, has anything on you. It's on page 108.

—*The Editors*

Middle C

About the Stickers

A set of peel-off stickers for the keys of your piano or electronic keyboard is included with this book. The diagram above shows how to position them.

The numbered stickers are primarily for electronic keyboard players who can't read music. If you are in this category, you will be playing the top line of the music, printed in blue. These are the treble, or right-hand, notes.

The lettered stickers are for two octaves of notes in the bass, or left-hand, clef — to the left of Middle C — on both electronic keyboards and pianos.

To position the labels of the right-hand notes on your instrument, first find Middle C, which will be Number 1. It is in the center, or just to the left of center, of the keyboard, the first white key below the grouping of two black keys.

Then the black key directly up from C, or C sharp (C♯) (which is the same as D flat [D♭]), becomes 1+. D becomes 2. D sharp (D♯), the same as E flat (E♭), becomes 2+, and so on, following the diagram.

Notes in the bass clef are identified by their letter names rather than by numbers. Position them as shown on the diagram. Starting on the C two octaves below Middle C, the white keys will read C-D-E-F-G-A-B and repeat again up to 1 (Middle C). The black keys will read C♯/D♭, D♯/E♭, F♯/G♭, G♯/A♭, A♯/B♭, until you reach the F♯/G♭, G♯/A♭ and A♯/B♭ just to the left of Middle C. The stickers will identify these as F+, G+ and A+. The reason for this is that the melody sometimes reaches down to those keys below Middle C, and, for non-music-readers, this is consistent with the 1+, 2+ identifications of the melody from Middle C upward.

Words and Music by Johnny Mercer

Slow and steady

TEMPO: Moderate   RHYTHM: Rhumba, Bossa Nova   COLOR: Strings, Flute

Dream a Little Dream of Me

Words by Gus Kahn; Music by Wilbur Schwandt and Fabian Andre

TEMPO: Moderately slow   RHYTHM: Swing, Disco   COLOR: Vibraphone, Clarinet

I Left My Heart in San Francisco

Words by Douglass Cross; Music by George Cory

TEMPO: Moderate   RHYTHM: Bossa Nova   COLOR: Electric Piano

IN THE MOOD

Music by Joseph Garland

Lindy (♫ played as ♪³♪)   TEMPO: Moderate   RHYTHM: Swing, Big Band   COLOR: Reed ensemble, Sax or Brass ensemble

LOVE LETTERS IN THE SAND

Words by Nick and Charles Kenny; Music by J. Fred Coots

TEMPO: Slow   RHYTHM: Rock   COLOR: Rock Guitar

Slowly

On a day like to-day, we passed the time a-

way writ-ing love let-ters in the sand. How you

laughed when I cried each time I saw the tide take our

love let-ters in the sand. You made a

Words by Johnny Burke; Music by Erroll Garner

TEMPO: Slow   RHYTHM: Slow Rock, Bossa Nova   COLOR: Jazz Organ, Strings

STAR DUST

SATIN DOLL

Words by Johnny Mercer;
Music by Duke Ellington and Billy Strayhorn

TEMPO: Moderately fast   RHYTHM: Swing, Big Band   COLOR: Jazz Organ, Piano

Moderate swing

Seems Like Old Times

Words and Music by Carmen Lombardo and John Jacob Loeb

TEMPO: Moderate   RHYTHM: Swing, Big Band   COLOR: Sax, Clarinet, Flute

IT'S ALL IN THE GAME

Words by Carl Sigman; Music by Charles Gates Dawes

Moderately slow

TEMPO: Moderately slow   RHYTHM: Waltz   COLOR: Celeste, Vibraphone

Too Young

Words by Sylvia Dee; Music by Sid Lippman

TEMPO: Moderate   RHYTHM: Big Band, Rhumba   COLOR: Vibraphone, Accordion

Words and Music by Bart Howard

TEMPO: Moderately slow   RHYTHM: Waltz   COLOR: Strings, Flute

AUTUMN LEAVES

English words by Johnny Mercer; Music by Joseph Kosma   French words by Jacques Prévert

TEMPO: Moderate   RHYTHM: Rhumba, Bossa Nova   COLOR: Strings, Flute

Moderately

The fall-ing leaves drift by the win-dow, the au-tumn leaves of red and gold. I see your lips, the sum-mer kiss-es,

IT'S A SIN TO TELL A LIE

Words and Music by Billy Mayhew

With a lilt

TEMPO: Moderate   RHYTHM: Swing, Big Band   COLOR: Saxophone, Accordion

Be sure it's true when you say "I love you." It's a sin to tell a lie.

Mil-lions of hearts have been bro - ken

just be-cause these words were spo - ken. I love

I'm Gonna Sit Right Down and Write Myself a Letter

Words by Joe Young; Music by Fred E. Ahlert

Moderate swing

TEMPO: Moderate to Fast   RHYTHM: Swing, Big Band   COLOR: Jazz Organ, Honkytonk Piano, Guitar

ALL OF ME

Words and Music by Seymour Simons and Gerald Marks

TEMPO: Moderate to Fast   RHYTHM: Swing, Big Band   COLOR: Brass ensemble

Red Sails in the Sunset

Words by Jimmy Kennedy; Music by Hugh Williams

TEMPO: Moderate   RHYTHM: Rhumba, Slow Rock   COLOR: Strings, Flute, Harmonica

The Very Thought of You

Words and Music by Ray Noble

Moderately slow, with a lilt

TEMPO: Moderately slow RHYTHM: Big Band, Swing COLOR: Clarinet, Flute

I Found a Million Dollar Baby
(in a Five and Ten Cent Store)

Words by Billy Rose and Mort Dixon; Music by Harry Warren

TEMPO: Moderate   RHYTHM: Big Band, Swing   COLOR: Sax, Trombone

These Foolish Things
(Remind Me of You)

Words by Holt Marvell; Music by Jack Strachey and Harry Link

TEMPO: Very slow   RHYTHM: Big Band, Swing   COLOR: Strings, Organ

TENDERLY

Words by Jack Lawrence; Music by Walter Gross

TEMPO: Very slow   RHYTHM: Waltz   COLOR: Strings

Lyrics:

The eve-ning breeze ca-ressed the trees ten-der-ly. The trem-bling trees em-braced the breeze ten-der-ly. Then you and I came wan-der-ing by, and lost in a sigh were we. The shore was

FOOLS RUSH IN

Words by Johnny Mercer; Music by Rube Bloom

TEMPO: Moderate   RHYTHM: Rhumba (Beguine)   COLOR: Flute, Strings

WHAT'S NEW?

Words by Johnny Burke; Music by Bob Haggart

TEMPO: Moderately slow   RHYTHM: Beguine, Big Band   COLOR: Trumpet, Strings

You Go to My Head

Words by Haven Gillespie; Music by J. Fred Coots

TEMPO: Slow   RHYTHM: Rhumba, Bossa Nova   COLOR: Flute, Clarinet, Horn

All The Things You Are

From *Very Warm for May*

Words by Oscar Hammerstein II; Music by Jerome Kern

TEMPO: Moderate to Fast   RHYTHM: Big Band, Bossa Nova   COLOR: Jazz Organ, Sax, Clarinet

Embraceable You

From *Girl Crazy*   Words by Ira Gershwin; Music by George Gershwin

TEMPO: Slow   RHYTHM: Swing, Bossa Nova   COLOR: Strings, Sax

Em - brace me, my sweet em - brace - a - ble you.

Em - brace me, you ir - re - place - a - ble you.

Just one look at you, my heart grew tip - sy in me.

You and you a - lone bring out the gyp - sy in me.

Tea for Two

From *No, No, Nanette*   Words by Irving Caesar; Music by Vincent Youmans

TEMPO: Moderately slow   RHYTHM: Pops, Cha Cha   COLOR: Muted Trumpet

With a lilt

NIGHT AND DAY

From *The Gay Divorce*   Words and Music by Cole Porter

TEMPO: Moderate   RHYTHM: Rhumba, Beguine   COLOR: Strings, Flute

I'VE GOT A CRUSH ON YOU

From *Treasure Girl* and *Strike Up the Band*   Words by Ira Gershwin; Music by George Gershwin

TEMPO: Moderately slow   **RHYTHM:** Swing   **COLOR:** Sax, Piano

I've got a crush on you, sweet-ie pie, all the day and night-time hear me sigh. I nev-er had the least no - tion that I could fall with so much e-mo - tion. Could you coo? Could you care for a cun-ning cot - tage we could share? The world will par-don my mush 'cause I've got a crush, my ba-by, on you.

April in Paris

From *Walk a Little Faster*

Words by E. Y. Harburg; Music by Vernon Duke

TEMPO: Slow to Moderate   RHYTHM: Swing   COLOR: Clarinet, Sax

HELLO, DOLLY!

From *Hello, Dolly!*   Words and Music by Jerry Herman

TEMPO: Fast   RHYTHM: Swing, Big Band   COLOR: Trumpet, Reed Synth.

YOU DO SOMETHING TO ME

From *Fifty Million Frenchmen*   Words and Music by Cole Porter

TEMPO: Fast   RHYTHM: Swing   COLOR: Piano, Jazz Organ

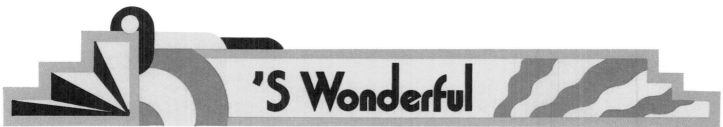

'S Wonderful

From *Funny Face*   Words by Ira Gershwin; Music by George Gershwin

TEMPO: Moderately fast   RHYTHM: Swing, Big Band   COLOR: Jazz Organ, **Trumpet**

Moderately fast

'S won-der – ful, _____ 's mar – vel – ous, _____

you should care _____ for _____ me. _____

'S aw – ful nice, _____ 's par – a – dise, _____

's what I love _____ to _____ see. _____ You've

The Man I Love

From *Strike Up the Band*   Words by Ira Gershwin; Music by George Gershwin

Slowly

TEMPO: Very slow   RHYTHM: Swing or Pops, or no rhythm   COLOR: Flute, Oboe, Accordion

Lyrics:

Some-day he'll come a-long, the man I love; And he'll be big and strong, the man I love;

And when he comes my way, I'll do my best to make him stay.

He'll look at me and smile, I'll un-der-stand; And in a lit-tle while he'll take my hand;

And though it seems ab-surd, I know we both won't say a word.

Dancing in the Dark

From *The Band Wagon*

Words by Howard Dietz; Music by Arthur Schwartz

TEMPO: Moderate   RHYTHM: Swing, Big Band   COLOR: Jazz Organ, Sax, Jazz Guitar

Lyrics:
Danc – ing in the dark till the tune ends, we're
danc – ing in the dark, and it soon ends; We're
waltz – ing in the won – der of why we're here;
Time hur – ries by, we're here and gone.

DANCING ON THE CEILING

From *Ever Green*   Words by Lorenz Hart; Music by Richard Rodgers

TEMPO: Moderately slow   RHYTHM: Cha Cha, Pops   COLOR: Muted trumpet, Flute

September Song

From *Knickerbocker Holiday*   *Words by Maxwell Anderson; Music by Kurt Weill*

Moderately slow

TEMPO: Moderately slow   RHYTHM: Bossa Nova or Beguine   COLOR: Cello

Smoke Gets In Your Eyes

From *Roberta*   Words by Otto Harbach; Music by Jerome Kern

TEMPO: Slow   RHYTHM: None, play freely   COLOR: Strings

With a Song in My Heart

From *Spring Is Here* Words by Lorenz Hart; Music by Richard Rodgers

TEMPO: Moderate RHYTHM: Rhumba, Big Band COLOR: Flute, Strings

My Heart Stood Still

From *A Connecticut Yankee*

Words by Lorenz Hart; Music by Richard Rodgers

TEMPO: Moderate   RHYTHM: Rhumba, Beguine   COLOR: Strings, Flute

Love Me or Leave Me

From *Whoopee*   Words by Gus Kahn; Music by Walter Donaldson

TEMPO: Moderately fast   RHYTHM: Swing, Big Band   COLOR: Sax, Trombone

LOVER, COME BACK TO ME

From *The New Moon*   Words by Oscar Hammerstein II; Music by Sigmund Romberg

TEMPO: Slow   RHYTHM: 16 Beat   COLOR: Strings

Stouthearted Men

From *The New Moon*   Words by Oscar Hammerstein II; Music by Sigmund Romberg

March tempo   TEMPO: Moderate   RHYTHM: March; or manually strike chord note on every beat   COLOR: Trumpet

Someone to Watch Over Me

From Oh, Kay! Words by Ira Gershwin; Music by George Gershwin

TEMPO: Slow RHYTHM: Rhumba or Pops COLOR: Flute or Strings

SEND IN THE CLOWNS

From *A Little Night Music*   Words and Music by Stephen Sondheim

TEMPO: Moderate   RHYTHM: Rhumba   COLOR: Guitar

Send In the Clowns

100

TOMORROW

From *Annie*   Words by Martin Charnin; Music by Charles Strouse

TEMPO: Medium fast   RHYTHM: Pops   COLOR: Clarinet

105
ALL THE WAY

"All the Way" went all the way to Best Film Song of 1957 and a million-selling recording for Frank Sinatra. Sammy Cahn and Jimmy Van Heusen wrote it for Sinatra to sing in *The Joker Is Wild*, the life story of Joe E. Lewis.

108
AS TIME GOES BY

Oh, come on. You *must* remember this. Morocco, 1941. Rick's Café Américain. Bergman and Bogart, and Dooley Wilson playing "As Time Goes By." Movies don't come any better than *Casablanca*, and songs don't come any better than this one.

110
BORN FREE

John Barry is best known for his brassy, rhythmic scores for such James Bond films as *Goldfinger* and *Thunderball*. He proved he could write softer stuff when he composed this sweeping Oscar-winning theme for *Born Free* (1966), a tremendous hit for pianist Roger Williams.

112
WHEN YOU WISH UPON A STAR

It's trivia time! Who sang this Academy Award-winning song in Walt Disney's *Pinocchio* in 1940? Give up? It was Jiminy Cricket, with a voice supplied by Cliff "Ukulele Ike" Edwards, a vaudeville star of the 1920s.

114
THREE COINS IN THE FOUNTAIN

Romance in Rome was the theme of *Three Coins in the Fountain*, and Sammy Cahn and Jule Styne came up with the perfect title song (an Oscar-winner) for the 1954 film. The "fountain" is the Fontana di Trevi. Legend has it that anyone who throws a coin into its waters is bound to return to the Eternal City. Try it and see.

116
DAYS OF WINE AND ROSES

It's a sad story, more about wine than roses. But the 1962 movie, starring Jack Lemmon and Lee Remick, will be remembered forever, thanks in part to Henry Mancini and Johnny Mercer's bittersweet Oscar-winning title theme.

118
I ONLY HAVE EYES FOR YOU

Harry Warren and Al Dubin wrote many film scores together—*42nd Street*, *Gold Diggers of 1933* and *Dames* among them—all containing many wonderful songs. Dick Powell sang "I Only Have Eyes for You" to Ruby Keeler in *Dames* (1934).

120
THE GLORY OF LOVE

Boston-born Billy Hill is known for his cowboy tunes—"The Last Roundup," "Wagon Wheels" and "Empty Saddles" among them—but his Eastern upbringing came through on "The Glory of Love." The song first became popular in 1936, hit again in 1967 after it it was used in *Guess Who's Coming to Dinner*, and yet again in 1989 when Bette Midler sang it in *Beaches*.

122
IT'S MAGIC

Doris Day made her reputation as a big-band singer with Les Brown and His Orchestra. Sammy Cahn and Jule Styne suggested her for a role in *Romance on the High Seas* (1948), in which she sang the composers' magical "It's Magic," and the rest is Hollywood history.

124
THEME FROM *A SUMMER PLACE*

Max Steiner's theme was the best thing about the soapy *A Summer Place* (1959). It became a best-selling recording for Percy Faith and His Orchestra—a recording that is to summer what Bing Crosby's "White Christmas" is to Christmas.

126
SEPTEMBER IN THE RAIN

Those leaves of brown have been tumbling down since 1937, when singer James Melton sang this lovely song in *Melody for Two*. It's another in the series of film tunes by the team of Harry Warren and Al Dubin.

128
THE WAY WE WERE

Just remember: We're not getting older, we're getting better. But it's always fun to look back on the way we were. Alan and Marilyn Bergman and Marvin Hamlisch's fond glance at the past, the title song of the Barbra Streisand–Robert Redford film, won an Oscar as Best Song of the Year in 1973.

131
THAT'S ALL

Among the records New York disc jockey–songwriter Bob Haymes played on his show was one of a melody he had written, called "C'est Tout." A fan call from Nat King Cole prompted Haymes to ask his friend Alan Brandt to supply lyrics for the tune. The result was this fine song, a fine recording for Cole and a fine addition to *Tootsie* 30 years later, in 1982.

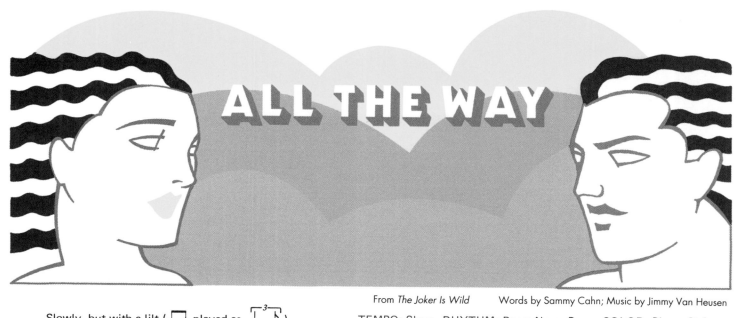

ALL THE WAY

From *The Joker Is Wild*   Words by Sammy Cahn; Music by Jimmy Van Heusen

AS TIME GOES BY

From *Casablanca*   Words and Music by Herman Hupfeld

TEMPO: Slow   RHYTHM: Big Band, Swing   COLOR: Sax, Piano

BORN FREE

From *Born Free*   Words by Don Black; Music by John Barry

TEMPO: Moderate   RHYTHM: Rhumba or Beguine   COLOR: Flute, Strings, Guitar

111

When You Wish Upon a Star

From *Pinocchio* Words by Ned Washington; Music by Leigh Harline

TEMPO: Slow RHYTHM: 16 beat COLOR: Strings

Three Coins in the Fountain

From *Three Coins in the Fountain*

Words by Sammy Cahn; Music by Jule Styne

TEMPO: Moderate   RHYTHM: Bossa Nova   COLOR: Oboe, Strings

Quietly

(music notation)

Three coins in the foun-tain, each one seek-ing hap-pi-ness,

thrown by three hope-ful lov-ers, which one will the foun-tain bless?

Three hearts in the foun-tain, each heart long-ing for its home;

There they lie in the foun-tain, some-where in the heart of Rome.

Days of Wine and Roses

From *Days of Wine and Roses* Words by Johnny Mercer; Music by Henry Mancini

TEMPO: Moderate RHYTHM: Rhumba, Beguine COLOR: Strings

Moderate Ballad

The days of wine and ros - es laugh and run a - way like a child at play, through the mead - ow - land to - ward a clos - ing door, a door marked "nev - er - more," that was - n't there be - fore. The

I ONLY HAVE EYES FOR YOU

From Dames   Words by Al Dubin; Music by Harry Warren

TEMPO: Moderate   RHYTHM: Rhumba (Beguine)   COLOR: Strings

THE GLORY OF LOVE

From *Guess Who's Coming to Dinner*   Words and Music by William Hill

With a lilt

TEMPO: Moderate   RHYTHM: Swing, Big Band   COLOR: Trumpet, Sax, Jazz Organ

IT'S MAGIC

From *Romance on the High Seas*   Words by Sammy Cahn; Music by Jule Styne

TEMPO: Slow   RHYTHM: Bossa Nova   COLOR: Flute, Piano

THEME FROM
A SUMMER PLACE

Words by Mack Discant; Music by Max Steiner

September in the Rain

From *Melody for Two*
Words by Al Dubin; Music by Harry Warren

TEMPO: Moderate   RHYTHM: Swing, Bossa Nova   COLOR: Brass Ensemble

ev - 'ry word of love I heard you whis - per,_____ the
rain-drops seemed to play a sweet re - frain._____ Though
spring is here to me it's still Sep - tem - ber,_____ that Sep-
tem - ber,_____ in the rain._____

THE WAY WE WERE

From *The Way We Were* Words by Alan and Marilyn Bergman; Music by Marvin Hamlisch

TEMPO: Slow RHYTHM: Disco, 16 beat COLOR: Piano, Organ

That's All

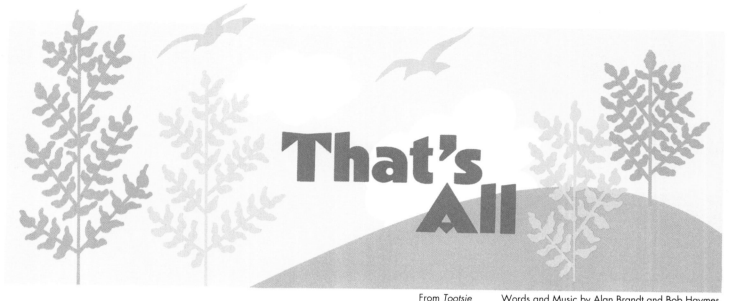

From *Tootsie*   Words and Music by Alan Brandt and Bob Haymes
TEMPO: Slow   RHYTHM: Pops, Big Band   COLOR: Strings, Piano

Very slowly, with expression

Lyrics:
I can on - ly give you love that lasts for - ev - er _____ and the prom-ise to be near each time you call, and the on - ly heart I own for you and you a - lone, that's all, that's all. I can

135
I DON'T KNOW WHY (I JUST DO)
In 1931, the great songwriting team of Fred Ahlert and Roy Turk turned out "Where the Blue of the Night (Meets the Gold of the Day)," which Bing Crosby co-wrote and made his theme song, and "I Don't Know Why"—which sparkled even brighter and oftener because *everybody* sang it.

136
MEAN TO ME
Here's another hit by Ahlert and Turk. Written in 1929, it was one of the last great torch songs of the '20s. Not surprisingly, it was a hit for the two great torch singers of the period, Helen Morgan and Ruth Etting.

138
YOU MADE ME LOVE YOU
Songwriters Joe McCarthy and James Monaco made us love this song—ever since 1913, when Al Jolson introduced it on Broadway. Judy Garland sang it in *Broadway Melody of 1938*, and Harry James recorded it in 1941, with hints of both Jolson and Garland in his trumpet phrasing.

140
FOR ME AND MY GAL
Songwriters can be businessmen too, you know. When George W. Meyer was asked why he composed "For Me and My Gal" in 1917 (along with Edgar Leslie and E. Ray Goetz), he answered, "I was writing songs for a living and I needed the money." By the way, lyricist Leslie borrowed the title from the last line of another golden oldie, "Shine On, Harvest Moon."

142
DANNY BOY
Here's a song that has brought a tear to many an eye—and not just Irish ones. The melody became known as "Londonderry Air" after it appeared in print for the first time in 1855 in a collection put together by a Miss J. Ross of Londonderry. It wasn't until 1912 that Fred E. Weatherly gave the air the words that made it "Danny Boy."

144
SIDE BY SIDE
Duos—of singers, comedians, dancers—have been performing "Side by Side" ever since Harry Woods wrote it in 1927. Kay Starr followed the trend when she made her hit recording in 1953. Her partner? Herself: she overdubbed her own voice.

146
MY BLUE HEAVEN
Composer Walter Donaldson was a bachelor when he and George Whiting wrote this paean to married life in 1927. The tune was a tremendous hit for singer Gene Austin that same year. The modest Austin once said: "The most important element in the success of a record is the song, not the singer. I got an old sayin': 'Hit songs don't care who sings 'em.' "

148
MY BUDDY
Walter Donaldson again, this time with lyricist Gus Kahn. The two clicked with this touching waltz, their first collaboration, in 1922. Realizing that they had a good thing going, they went on to create such other standards as "Carolina in the Morning," "Yes Sir, That's My Baby," "Makin' Whoopee" and "Love Me or Leave Me."

150
BYE BYE BLACKBIRD
Ray Henderson and Mort Dixon's "Bye Bye Blackbird" came along in 1926. The song—a favorite of singing comedians Eddie Cantor and Georgie Price—was one of 10 hits that Henderson wrote in 1925 and 1926, among them "The Birth of the Blues," "Five Foot Two," "Alabamy Bound," "I'm Sitting on Top of the World" and "Black Bottom."

152
APRIL SHOWERS
Buddy De Sylva wrote the words for three of Al Jolson's greatest hits—"Avalon," "California Here I Come" and "April Showers." Jolson introduced "April Showers" (the melody was by Louis Silvers) in the Broadway musical *Bombo* in 1921 and continued to sing it throughout his career.

154
POOR BUTTERFLY
John Golden wrote the lyrics of "Poor Butterfly" in 1916, basing them on the plot of Puccini's opera *Madama Butterfly*. (Raymond Hubbell supplied the melody.) Stage star Sophye Bernard's performance of the song in *The Big Show*, an extravaganza at New York City's Hippodrome, turned the graceful ballad into one of the era's biggest hits.

156
I'M LOOKING OVER A FOUR-LEAF CLOVER
Mort Dixon teamed with Harry Woods to write this happy, jaunty 1920s song. It's been a favorite of the banjo-and-mandolin bands that march in Philadelphia's annual Mummers' Parade ever since, and was a good-luck charm for bandleader Art Mooney, who copied the string bands' style for a hit recording in 1947.

158
ALEXANDER'S RAGTIME BAND
Can you name five songs written by the great Irving Berlin that begin with the letter A? Hint: "Alexander's Ragtime Band" was the first one...way back in 1911. Others that you're sure to know are "All Alone," "All by Myself," "Anything You Can Do" and the immortal "Always."

160
ARE YOU LONESOME TONIGHT?
What is a country song like "Are You Lonesome Tonight?" doing in a group of old-time tunes, you ask? Well, sure, Elvis Presley had a huge hit with it in 1960, but in fact the song was written back in 1926 by Tin Pan Alley veterans Roy Turk and Lou Handman, who probably had no idea what "country music" was.

162
TILL WE MEET AGAIN
This charming waltz by Richard Whiting and Raymond Egan, published in 1918, was one of the hit songs of World War I. It was the first of a string of successes by composer Whiting (father of singer Margaret) that included "The Japanese Sandman," "Sleepy Time Gal" and "Beyond the Blue Horizon."

164
SHINE ON, HARVEST MOON
Let's hope that vaudevillians Nora Bayes and Jack Norworth had some inkling that they were writing perhaps the ultimate singing-round-the-campfire song when they created "Shine On, Harvest Moon" in 1908. Norworth also wrote the words of another perennial seasonal favorite: "Take Me Out to the Ball Game."

165
TOO-RA-LOO-RA-LOO-RAL (THAT'S AN IRISH LULLABY)
Before there was Bing Crosby (who sang "Too-Ra-Loo-Ra-Loo-Ral" to that leprechaun of a priest, Barry Fitzgerald, in *Going My Way* in 1944), there was Chauncey Olcott. Singer-songwriter Olcott specialized in sentimental Irish airs. He popularized James Royce Shannon's "Irish lullaby" (in 1914) as well as his own classics, "My Wild Irish Rose," "When Irish Eyes Are Smiling" and "Mother Machree."

♪

I DON'T KNOW WHY

(I Just Do)

Words by Roy Turk; Music by Fred E. Ahlert

TEMPO: Moderately Slow   RHYTHM: Swing, Big Band   COLOR: Jazz Organ, Trombone

MEAN TO ME

Words and Music by Roy Turk and Fred E. Ahlert

TEMPO: Moderate   RHYTHM: Swing, Big Band   COLOR: Trumpet, Sax

Light and swingy

Lyrics:

You're mean to me. Why must you be mean to me? Gee, hon-ey, it seems to me you love to see me cry - in'. I don't know why I stay home each night when you say you'll phone; You don't and I'm left a - lone sing-in' the blues and sigh - in'. You treat me

YOU MADE ME LOVE YOU

Words by Joseph McCarthy; Music by James V. Monaco

Moderately, with a lilt (♩♩ played as ♩³♪)   TEMPO: Moderate   RHYTHM: Big Band, Swing   COLOR: Trumpet, Strings, Accordion

You made me love you. I did-n't want to do it; I did-n't want to do it.

You made me want you, and all the time you knew it; I guess you al-ways knew it.

You made me hap-py; Some-times you made me glad. But there were

times, dear, you made me feel so bad. You made me

For Me and My Gal

Words by Edgar Leslie and E. Ray Goetz; Music by George W. Meyer

TEMPO: Moderate   RHYTHM: Swing   COLOR: Strings

DANNY BOY

Words by Fred E. Weatherly; Music Traditional

TEMPO: Moderate   RHYTHM: Rhumba or Swing   COLOR: Flute, Strings

G(7) C F C
5 6 7 8 7 7 6 5 6 5 3 1
But come ye back when sum-mer's in the mea - dow,
D7 G7 C F C
mf
C G E F E G
G(7) Am F D(7)
5 6 7 8 7 7 6 5 3 2
or when the val - ley's hushed and white with snow.
D7 G7 Am F D7
C A E C F F♯ A A♭
G(7) C F C
5 5 5 10 9 9 8 6 8 5 3 1
It's I'll be here in sun-shine or in sha - dow;
G7 C E7 F C/E bass
f
G B C G C G♯ A E E
F C G(7) C
B 1 2 3 6 5 3 2 1 A B 1
Oh, Dan-ny boy, oh, Dan-ny boy, I love you so.
F D7/F♯ C/G C/E F6 G7 C
p
F F♯ G E F G C G C

SIDE BY SIDE

Words and Music by Harry Woods

TEMPO: Moderate   RHYTHM: Big Band, Swing   COLOR: Banjo, Honkytonk Piano

Oh, we ain't got a bar-rel of mon - ey, may - be we're rag-ged and fun - ny, but we'll trav-el a - long sing-in' a song side by side.

Don't know what's com-in' to - mor - row, may - be it's trou-ble and sor - row, but we'll trav-el the road shar-in' our load side by side.

MY BLUE HEAVEN

Words by George Whiting; Music by Walter Donaldson

TEMPO: Moderately fast   RHYTHM: Big Band   COLOR: Trumpet, Clarinet, Sax

My Buddy

Words by Gus Kahn; Music by Walter Donaldson

TEMPO: Moderately slow   RHYTHM: Waltz   COLOR: Music Box, Violin, Vibraphone

Nights are long since you went a - way, I think a - bout you all through the day, my bud - dy, my bud - dy, no bud - dy quite so true.

For a charming "music box" effect, play both hands an 8va higher.

Bye Bye Blackbird

Words by Mort Dixon; Music by Roy Henderson

Moderate singalong tempo   TEMPO: Moderate   RHYTHM: Big Band, Swing   COLOR: Trumpet, Clarinet, Trombone, Jazz Organ

Words by B.G. DeSylva; Music by Louis Silvers

TEMPO: Moderate   RHYTHM: Big Band, Swing   COLOR: Strings, Clarinet

POOR BUTTERFLY

Words by John L. Golden; Music by Raymond Hubbell

Moderately slow

TEMPO: Moderately slow   RHYTHM: Swing, Rhumba   COLOR: Strings, Flute

I'm Looking Over a Four-Leaf Clover

Words by Mort Dixon; Music by Harry Woods

TEMPO: Fast   RHYTHM: Big Band, Swing   COLOR: Trumpet, Banjo

Alexander's Ragtime Band

Words and Music by Irving Berlin

TEMPO: Moderately fast   RHYTHM: Swing, Big Band   COLOR: Sax, Jazz Organ

Are You Lonesome Tonight?

Words and Music by Roy Turk and Lou Handman

TEMPO: Moderate   RHYTHM: Waltz   COLOR: Organ, Strings

Moderately

Are you lone-some to-night? Do you miss me to-night? Are you sor-ry we drift-ed a-part? Does your mem-o-ry stray to a bright sum-mer day, when I kissed you and called you sweet-heart? Do the

TILL WE MEET AGAIN

Words by Raymond Egan; Music by Richard Whiting

Slow waltz

TEMPO: Slow to moderate   RHYTHM: Waltz   COLOR: Strings, Harmonica or Accordion

SHINE ON, HARVEST MOON

Words and Music by Nora Bayes and Jack Norworth

TEMPO: Moderate   RHYTHM: Big Band, Swing   COLOR: Banjo, Harmonica

TOO-RA-LOO-RA-LOO-RAL

(That's an Irish Lullaby)

Words and Music by James Royce Shannon

Moderately, with expression

TEMPO: Moderate   RHYTHM: Disco   COLOR: Panpipe, Flute

INSPIRATIONAL, COUNTRY AND FOLK FAVORITES

167
AMAZING GRACE

John Newton's poem, written as part of a sermon in 1779, has become one of the most popular hymns of all time. Newton, by that time an ordained minister in the Anglican church, had been captain of a slave ship for many years—and was rescued from that life by the power of grace.

168
HOW GREAT THOU ART

Although it dates back more than 100 years, "How Great Thou Art" is one of the most recent—and most popular—of religious songs. It was written in 1886 by a Swedish missionary, but was not translated into English until 1948, by the Reverend Stuart K. Hine. It became popular in the 1950s, thanks to George Beverly Shea, who sang it often during the Billy Graham Crusades.

170
WHISPERING HOPE

We're indebted to Philadelphian Septimus Winner for such odes as "Where Oh Where Has My Little Dog Gone," "Listen to the Mocking Bird," "What Is Home Without a Mother?" and—in a more tranquil vein—"Whispering Hope." He published "Whispering Hope" in 1868, under his mother's maiden name, Alice Hawthorne, presumably thinking the song's tender sentiments more feminine than masculine.

172
ROCK OF AGES

Augustus Toplady's beloved hymn "Rock of Ages," written in 1776, has consistently been among the top five favorite gospel songs. It was set to its present tune by the American composer and teacher Thomas Hastings in 1832.

173
PRAISE GOD FROM WHOM ALL BLESSINGS FLOW

Thomas Ken, an Anglican bishop, was royal chaplain to one British king, prisoner in the Tower of London of another. He will always be remembered for this simple four-line stanza, which he wrote in 1674 for a prayer manual. The sturdy tune it is set to, called "Old Hundredth," was composed by Louis Bourgeois and published in 1551.

174
IN THE GARDEN

In 1912, C. Austin Miles experienced a spiritual vision in which he saw Mary Magdalene and Jesus in the Garden of Gethsemane, where Jesus was buried. Miles awoke from his trance inspired to write the poem for this timeless gospel favorite. He added the music that night.

175
SHENANDOAH

Was "Shenandoah" named for a river in Virginia, a valley, an Indian maid or an Indian chief? The origins of the haunting song are clouded by time. Over the past two centuries, different versions of it have been sung by lumberjacks, river-barge men and sailors on the original tall ships. Our thanks to all of them.

176
GOODNIGHT, IRENE

Huddie Ledbetter, or Leadbelly, the legendary singer-guitarist from Louisiana, learned "Goodnight, Irene" from his uncle. He had been singing it for years when he first recorded it, for a Library of Congress folk-song project, in 1933. Leadbelly always believed the song could become a hit. He died in 1949, a year before The Weavers' recording became just that.

178
GREENSLEEVES

Legend has it that the oft-married English king Henry VIII wrote "Greensleeves." Whether he did or not, it's a regal tune. At Christmastime, the hymn "What Child Is This?" is sung to the melody.

180
I CAN'T STOP LOVING YOU

Many Nashville songwriters strive for years to come up with a hit song; Don Gibson managed to write two country classics in one afternoon: "I Can't Stop Loving You" and "Oh, Lonesome Me." The songs provided Gibson with a double-sided No.1 hit in 1958. "I Can't Stop Loving You" was also a big success for another country singer, Kitty Wells, and for rhythm-and-blues star Ray Charles.

182
TENNESSEE WALTZ

Pee Wee King and Redd Stewart's "Tennessee Waltz" was one of the first country and western songs to become a pop music hit, thanks to Patti Page's 1950 recording. Even though it's about a broken romance, not about the virtues of Tennessee, the ballad is now the official song of the Volunteer State.

184
DON'T FENCE ME IN

Guess who takes credit for this tune of the wide-open spaces? None other than Yale man Cole Porter, one of the most sophisticated of composers. For the lyrics, though, Porter turned to a poem he had bought in the 1930s from a genuine rider of the purple sage—for $200.

AMAZING GRACE

Words by John Newton; Music Traditional

TEMPO: Moderate   RHYTHM: None (Use single finger bass)   COLOR: Bagpipe, Oboe
Note: If you have the Bagpipe sound on your keyboard, hold down the F and C keys with the left hand and play the melody with the right hand.

Additional Verses

How sweet the name of Jesus sounds
In a believer's ear;
It soothes his sorrows, heals his wounds,
And drives away his fear.

Must Jesus bear the cross alone
And all the world go free?
No, there's a cross for ev'ryone,
And there's a cross for me.

How Great Thou Art

English Words by Stuart K. Hine; Swedish Folk Melody

Additional Verses

And when I think that God, His Son not sparing,
Sent Him to die, I scarce can take it in;
That on the cross my burden gladly bearing,
He bled and died to take away my sin.
(Repeat Chorus)

When Christ shall come with shout of acclamation
And take me home, what joy shall fill my heart.
Then I shall bow in humble adoration
And there proclaim, my God, how great Thou art!
(Repeat Chorus)

Whispering Hope

Words and Music by Alice Hawthorne

Moderate waltz

TEMPO: Moderate   RHYTHM: Waltz (or none)   COLOR: Organ, Human Voice (Vox Humana)

※ *The last 16 measures are played twice.*

ROCK OF AGES

Words by Augustus M. Toplady; Music by Thomas Hastings
TEMPO: Moderately slow   RHYTHM: Waltz (or none)   COLOR: Organ

1. Rock of A - ges, cleft for me! Let me hide my - self in
2. Could my tears for - ev - er flow, could my zeal no lan - guor

(1) Thee; Let the wa - ter and the blood from Thy wound - ed side which
(2) know, Let these for sin could not a - tone; Thou must save and Thou a -

(1) flowed, be of sin the dou - ble cure: Save from wrath and make me pure.
(2) lone. In my hand no price I bring, sim - ply to Thy cross I cling.

Praise God from Whom All Blessings Flow

Words by Thomas Ken; Music by Louis Bourgeois

TEMPO: Slow and stately   RHYTHM: None   COLOR: Organ

IN THE GARDEN

Words and Music by C. Austin Miles

Very slowly in 2 (♩.= 1 beat)
or Moderately in 6 (♪ = 1 beat)

TEMPO: Slow   RHYTHM: Slow Gospel (Rock and Roll)   COLOR: Organ

1. I come to the gar-den a-lone, while the dew is still on the ros-es; And the
2. He speaks, and the sound of His voice is so sweet the birds hush their sing-ing; And the
3. I'd stay in the gar-den with Him though the night a-round me be fall-ing; But He

(1) voice I hear fall-ing on my ear, the Son of God dis-clos-es.
(2) mel-o-dy that He gave to me with-in my heart is ring-ing.   And He
(3) bids me go; Through the voice of woe, His voice to me is call-ing.

walks with me, and He talks with me, and He tells me I am His own; And the

joy we share as we tar-ry there, none oth-er has ev-er known.

SHENANDOAH

Traditional

Freely

TEMPO: Slow   RHYTHM: None, play freely   COLOR: Harmonica, Oboe

1. Oh, Shen-an-doah,___ I long to hear you,
2. Oh, Shen-an-doah,___ I love your daugh-ter, } A - way, you roll-ing
3. Oh, Shen-an-doah,___ I'm goin' to leave you,

(1) { Oh, Shen-an-doah,___ just to be near you,
riv-er. (2) { Oh, Shen-an-doah,___ a-cross the wa-ter, } A - way, we're bound a-
(3) { Oh, Shen-an-doah,___ I won't de-ceive you,

way,   'cross the   wide   Mis - sou - ri.   D.C.*

Repeat from the beginning for additional words.

Copyright © 1991 Padmi Publishing Co.

175

Goodnight, Irene

Words and Music by Huddie Ledbetter and John Lomax

TEMPO: Moderate   RHYTHM: Waltz   COLOR: Harmonica, Guitar

Moderate waltz

Chorus

I - rene, good - night;_____ I - rene, good - night._____ Good - night, I - rene; Good - night, I - rene; I'll see you in my dreams._____

GREENSLEEVES

Traditional

TEMPO: Moderate   RHYTHM: Waltz   COLOR: Recorder, Pan Flute

I CAN'T STOP LOVING YOU

Words and Music by Don Gibson

TEMPO: Moderate   RHYTHM: Country   COLOR: Strings, Rock Organ

Those hap-py hours that we once knew, though long a-go still make me blue. They say that time heals a bro-ken heart, but time has stood still since we've been a-part.

* This song begins on the 2nd beat of the measure.

Tennessee Waltz

Words and Music by Redd Stewart and Pee Wee King

Moderately slow waltz

TEMPO: Moderately slow   RHYTHM: Waltz   COLOR: Strings, Electric Guitar

I was waltz-ing with my dar-lin' to the Ten-nes-see Waltz when an old friend I hap-pened to see. In-tro-duced him to my loved one, and while they were waltz-ing, my friend stole my sweet-heart from me. I re-

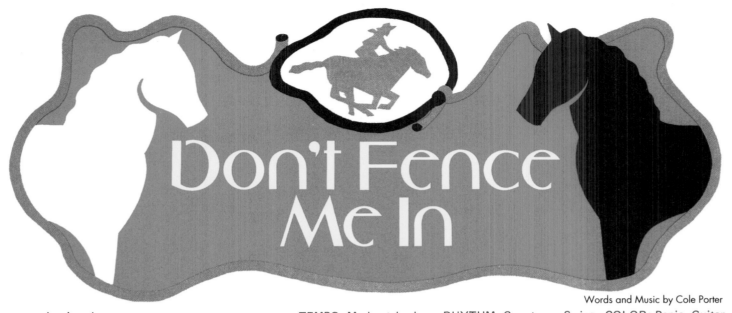

Don't Fence Me In

Words and Music by Cole Porter

TEMPO: Moderately slow   RHYTHM: Country or Swing   COLOR: Banjo, Guitar

Don't Fence Me In

188
GOD BLESS AMERICA

You know, "The Star-Spangled Banner" didn't officially become the national anthem of the United States until 1931. And if there's ever a referendum to replace it, one of the chief contenders will surely be Irving Berlin's hymn to his adopted country. The Russian-born composer never profited from this enduring classic. He donated all the royalties to the Boy Scouts and Girl Scouts of America.

190
AMERICA THE BEAUTIFUL

Katherine Lee Bates's "America the Beautiful" was a runner-up for U.S. national anthem back in 1931. Miss Bates was a professor of English who had been to Europe several times but hadn't seen much of her own country. When she made her first trip west, in 1893, she was awed by the view from the top of Pikes Peak in Colorado. She promptly wrote this stirring hymn of praise, which she elected to set to a stately tune by Samuel A. Ward.

191
THIS LAND IS YOUR LAND

In a sense, nobody ever really wrote this melody. Wandering minstrel Woody Guthrie adapted the music from two songs by the Carter Family, who in turn had borrowed the tune from an even older folk song. "This Land Is Your Land" was introduced by The Weavers in 1956 and helped to fire the folk music revival that soon followed.

192
DIXIE

"Dixie" has been a rallying cry for the South from Civil War days to the present, but the song was written by a Yankee, Ohio-born minstrel man Dan Emmett. In 1859, Emmett was performing with a troupe in New York City. As he sat in his boardinghouse one cold, rainy Sunday, trying to write a closing song for the show, the dismal weather made him wish he were "in the land of cotton." The rest is part of history.

194
BATTLE HYMN OF THE REPUBLIC

The Northern equivalent of "Dixie" during the Civil War was the work of Julia Ward Howe, a poet, abolitionist and suffragette. She wrote "Battle Hymn of the Republic"—to the same tune as "John Brown's Body"—after touring an army camp near Washington, D.C., in 1861. Her poem was published the following year in the *Atlantic Monthly*, and has been a source of inspiration ever since.

196
ANNIVERSARY SONG

Written in 1880 by Romanian composer Ion Ivanovici, "Danube Waves" has long been a favorite at Jewish weddings. In 1947, Al Jolson and Saul Chaplin tried to capture that atmosphere for the film *The Jolson Story* and turned "Danube Waves" into "Anniversary Song." Larry Parks played the "world's greatest entertainer" on-screen, but Jolson did his own singing on the soundtrack. His recording of "Anniversary Song" became a best-seller.

198
LET ME CALL YOU SWEETHEART

Leo Friedman and Beth Slater Whitson made a mistake with their first song: in 1909 they sold "Meet Me Tonight in Dreamland" outright to the publisher. They got a few dollars; the publisher reaped a fortune when the tune sold more than 2 million copies of sheet music. The composers struck a better bargain the following year for "Let Me Call You Sweetheart": this time they got royalties on the 5 million copies sold.

200
RUDOLPH THE RED-NOSED REINDEER

Robert L. May, a copywriter for Montgomery Ward, wrote a little story about a reindeer with a bright red nose in 1939. Ten years later, songwriter Johnny Marks took the tale of Rudolph and created a Christmas classic. Singing cowboy Gene Autry's 1949 recording sold more than 2 million copies.

202
WINTER WONDERLAND

Richard Smith and Felix Bernard wrote this cozy ballad about the wonders of wintertime in 1934, but it wasn't until 1950 that the song became popular, thanks to a recording by The Andrews Sisters. Since then, it's been a perennial favorite.

204
AULD LANG SYNE

Scottish poet Robert Burns created this hymn to "old long ago" in the late 18th century. For 150 years, it was simply a song of the parting of friends. Then, on New Year's Eve in 1929, Guy Lombardo decided to play it at midnight. The song became so associated with New Year's Eve and with Lombardo that the bandleader used to joke: "When I go, New Year's Eve goes with me." It hasn't been the same without him.

205
HAPPY DAYS ARE HERE AGAIN

"Happy Days Are Here Again" is one of the first Depression-era songs, although it was written early in 1929, before the stock market crash in October. Its use was ironic, but it helped to lift spirits in those grim years and became Franklin D. Roosevelt's campaign song in 1932. Barbra Streisand took it up and made it a hit again in 1963.

208
HAPPY BIRTHDAY TO YOU

No, people haven't been singing "Happy Birthday to You" for hundreds of years. Sisters Patty and Mildred Hill, kindergarten teachers in Louisville, Kentucky, wrote it in 1893. Because it wasn't copyrighted until 1935, however, the song still earns royalties—up to $1 million a year. Not surprisingly, the *Guinness Book of World Records* lists it as one of the three most popular songs in the English language (along with "Auld Lang Syne" and "For He's a Jolly Good Fellow").

GOD BLESS AMERICA

Words and Music by Irving Berlin

TEMPO: Moderately slow   RHYTHM: March   COLOR: Brass Ensemble, Strings, Organ

America the Beautiful

Words by Katherine Lee Bates; Music by Samuel Augustus Ward

TEMPO: Moderate   RHYTHM: None (or very slow march)   COLOR: Organ

THIS LAND IS YOUR LAND

Words and Music by Woody Guthrie

*This song begins on the 2nd beat of the measure.

Additional Verses

I've roamed and rambled, and I followed my footsteps
To the sparkling sands of her diamond deserts.
And all around me a voice was sounding,
This land was made for you and me.

When the sun comes shining and I was strolling,
And the wheat fields waving and the dust clouds rolling;
As the fog was lifting, a voice was chanting,
This land was made for you and me.

DIXIE

Words and Music by Daniel Decatur Emmett

TEMPO: Moderately slow   RHYTHM: March   COLOR: Brass Ensemble, Flute

Spirited March

BATTLE HYMN OF THE REPUBLIC

Words by Julia Ward Howe; Music by William Steffe

Moderately slow march   TEMPO: Moderately slow   RHYTHM: March or without rhythm   COLOR: Organ, Brass Choir, Trumpet
(repeat chord on each beat)

1. Mine eyes have seen the glo - ry of the com - ing of the Lord; He is
2. I have seen Him in the watch fires of a hun - dred cir - cling camps, they have

(1) tram - pling out the vin - tage where the grapes of wrath are stored; He hath
(2) build - ed Him an al - tar in the eve - ning dews and damps, I can

(1) loosed the fate - ful light - ning of His ter - ri - ble swift sword; His
(2) read His right - eous sen - tence by the dim and flar - ing lamps; His

Additional Verses

He has sounded forth the trumpet that shall never sound retreat;
He is sifting out the hearts of men before His judgment seat;
O be swift, my soul, to answer Him! Be jubilant, my feet!
Our God is marching on.
(Chorus)

In the beauty of the lilies, Christ was born across the sea,
With a glory in His bosom that transfigures you and me.
As He died to make men holy, let us die to make men free,
While God is marching on.
(Chorus)

ANNIVERSARY SONG

Words by Al Jolson; Music by Saul Chaplin

TEMPO: Moderate   RHYTHM: Waltz   COLOR: Strings, Cello

Repeat from the beginning and play through to the word "Fine." Use the second set of words.

197

LET ME CALL YOU SWEETHEART

Words by Beth Slater Whitson; Music by Leo Friedman

TEMPO: Moderate   RHYTHM: Waltz   COLOR: Strings, Organ

Copyright © 1991 Ardee Mus. Pub. Inc. In Canada: Copyright © 1910 by Leo Friedman. Copyright Renewed and Assigned to Shawnee Press, Inc., Pennsylvania, and Shapiro, Bernstein & Co. Inc., New York. Published by Shawnee Press, Inc., and Shapiro, Bernstein & Co. Inc. Used by Permission.

RUDOLPH THE RED-NOSED REINDEER

Words and Music by Johnny Marks

Moderately

TEMPO: Moderate to Fast   RHYTHM: Country or Swing   COLOR: Toy or Electric Piano, Vibraphone

Ru-dolph the Red-Nosed Rein-deer had a ver-y shin-y nose,

and if you ev-er saw it, you could e-ven say it glows. All of the oth-er

rein-deer used to laugh and call him names; They nev-er let poor

Ru-dolph join in an-y rein-deer games. Then one fog-gy

WINTER WONDERLAND

Words by Richard Smith; Music by Felix Bernard

TEMPO: Moderate   RHYTHM: Big Band, Swing   COLOR: Strings, Accordion, Guitar

202

Auld Lang Syne

Words by Robert Burns; Music Traditional

Firmly   TEMPO: Moderately   RHYTHM: None, or March   COLOR: Brass Choir, Organ or Bagpipe

Should auld ac-quaint-ance be for - got and nev – er brought to mind? Should

auld ac-quaint - ance be for - got and days of auld lang syne. For

auld____ lang____ syne, my dear, for auld____ lang____ syne; We'll

take a cup of kind - ness yet for auld____ lang____ syne.

Happy Days Are Here Again

Words by Jack Yellen; Music by Milton Ager

With a lift

TEMPO: Fast   RHYTHM: March/Polka   COLOR: Trumpet, Brass Ensemble

Words and Music by Mildred J. Hill and Patty Smith Hill

TEMPO: Moderate   RHYTHM: Waltz   COLOR: Piano, Accordion